KINGFISHER READERS

level **2**

D1065796

Birds of Prey

Claire Llewellyn

KINGFISHER

NEW YORK

KINGFISHER
LONDON & NEW YORK

Copyright © Macmillan Publishers International Ltd 2017
Published in the United States by Kingfisher,
175 Fifth Ave., New York, NY 10010
Kingfisher is an imprint of Pan Macmillan, London.
All rights reserved.

Distributed in the U.S. and Canada by Macmillan,
175 Fifth Ave., New York, NY 10010

Library of Congress Cataloging-in-Publication Data

Names: Llewellyn, Claire.
Title: Birds of prey / Claire Llewellyn.
Description: New York : Kingfisher, 2017. | Series: Kingfisher readers. Level
  2 | Audience: Age 6. | Audience: Grades K to 3.
Identifiers: LCCN 2016049241| ISBN 9780753473412 (hardback) | ISBN
  9780753473429 (pbk.)
Subjects: LCSH: Birds of prey--Juvenile literature.
Classification: LCC QL677.78 .L55 2017 | DDC 598.9--dc23
LC record available at https://lccn.loc.gov/2016049241

Series editor: Thea Feldman
Literacy consultant: Ellie Costa, Bank Street College, New York
Design: Peter Clayman

978-0-7534-7341-2 (HB)
978-0-7534-7342-9 (PB)

Kingfisher books are available for special promotions
and premiums. For details contact: Special Markets
Department, Macmillan, 175 Fifth Ave., New York, NY 10010.

For more information, please visit
www.kingfisherbooks.com

Printed in China

9 8 7 6 5 4 3 2 1

1TR/0317/WKT/UG/105MA

Picture credits
The Publisher would like to thank the following for permission to reproduce their material.
Top = t; Bottom = b; Center = c; Left = l; Right = r
Cover iStock/Kandfoto; Pages 4–5 iStock/Dgwildlife; 5t Shutterstock/Dennis W Donohue;
6 Shutterstock/Glass and Nature; 6–7 iStock/Byrdyak; 7 Shutterstock/Martin-Kubik;
8 Shutterstock/Alexey Stiop; 9t iStock/MonteComeau, 9m iStock/James Pintar; 10–11
Shutterstock/Keneva Photography; 12 iStock/Lakes4life; 13t flpa/Photo Researchers, 13b
iStock/Mark-paton; 14 iStock/cadifor, 14–15 iStock/Holcy; 15 Nature Picture Library/Nick
Garbutt; 16–17 Getty/Minden Pictures; 17 iStock/kajornyot; 18 iStock/jimkruger, 18–19 iStock/
cnmacdon; 20, 21t, 21b iStock/Bousfield; 22t iStock/Anagramm, 22–23 iStock/ottoduplessis; 24
Getty/PREAU Louis-Marie/hemis.fr; 25t iStock/Lokibaho, 25b Shutterstock/Juha Saastamoinen;
26 Getty/Auscape/Contributor; 27 Getty/Wayne Lynch; 28b iStock/ Brian Balster, 28–29 iStock/
fotokostic; 29t iStock/ozflash; 30 iStock/Beka_C; 31t iStock/mzphoto11, 31b Shutterstock/
Katiekk.

Contents

What are birds of prey?

Birds of **prey** are birds that hunt and eat other animals.

A bird of prey has
a hooked beak,
sharp claws,
and **keen** eyesight.

Meet birds of prey

There are about 450 kinds of birds of prey.

Falcons, vultures, owls, and eagles are some kinds of birds of prey.

kestrel

boreal owl

Most birds of prey
look for animals
to catch and eat.

vulture

Where are they?

Birds of prey live all over the world in many different **habitats**.

desert eagle
owl

They live in deserts, **grasslands**, and rain forests.

They live by lakes, rivers, and coasts.

osprey

snowy owl

They live in mountains, cold forests, and the icy Arctic.

Birds of prey live everywhere except for Antarctica.

A hunter's body

A bird of prey's body is built for hunting.

Long, sharp claws called **talons** grab and grip prey tightly.

Strong eyes
spot prey
down below.

Curved, sharp
beak tears
into prey.

Strong wings
lift a bird of prey
high into the air.

red-tailed kite

11

Danger in the sky

Some birds of prey, including falcons and hawks, eat other birds.

A kestrel is a kind of falcon.

kestrel

peregrine
falcon

The peregrine falcon sees a bird
and dives down to catch it.

It grabs the bird in midair!

peregrine
falcon

What do they eat?

Many birds of prey eat rabbits, mice, and **voles**.

Some eat lizards and snakes.

common buzzard

Other birds of prey catch snails, crabs, and fish.

red-tailed hawk

harpy
eagle

This harpy eagle snatched
a monkey from the treetops
in the rain forests of South
America.

barn owl

Night hunters

Owls hunt at night.

An owl flies without
making a sound.

pygmy owl

Its prey does not see
or hear it coming.

Owls use their large eyes
to see very well in the dark.

Snowy owls

The snowy owl's thick feathers
keep it warm in the Arctic.

Its feathers also help the owl
blend in with the snow
and hide from prey.

The snowy owl hunts **hares** and **lemmings**.

The owl can hear a lemming under the snow, and dives to catch it!

Fishing birds

An osprey spots a fish
and dives into the water.

Its talons grab the slippery prey!

Then the osprey flies
back up into the air.

Vultures

Vultures eat animals
that are already dead.

A group of vultures
spreads out in the
sky until one spots
a **carcass**.

Vultures do not have feathers on their heads.

This helps them keep clean when they dig into a carcass.

Nesting time

Some birds of prey build nests on rocky ledges.

Others build nests in trees.

eagle owl chicks

great horned owl

The female bird lays the eggs and sits on them for up to eight weeks.

osprey

The male hunts for food and keeps other birds away.

Growing up

A newborn bird of prey cannot fly or hunt for food.

Its parents bring it food.

kestrel chick

A young bird will learn to hunt and to fly before it leaves the nest.

Most young birds of prey leave home before they are five months old.

great gray owl and chick

Birds in danger

All over the world, birds of prey are losing their habitats.

People are taking over the land where birds of prey live.

People are building homes and farms on the land.

Many farmers spray their crops to poison insects and other **pests**.

When birds of prey
eat the pests,
they get sick too.

barn
owl

Protecting birds

Scientists are helping to protect birds of prey in different ways.

Some scientists **breed** chicks and set them free in the wild.

vulture chick

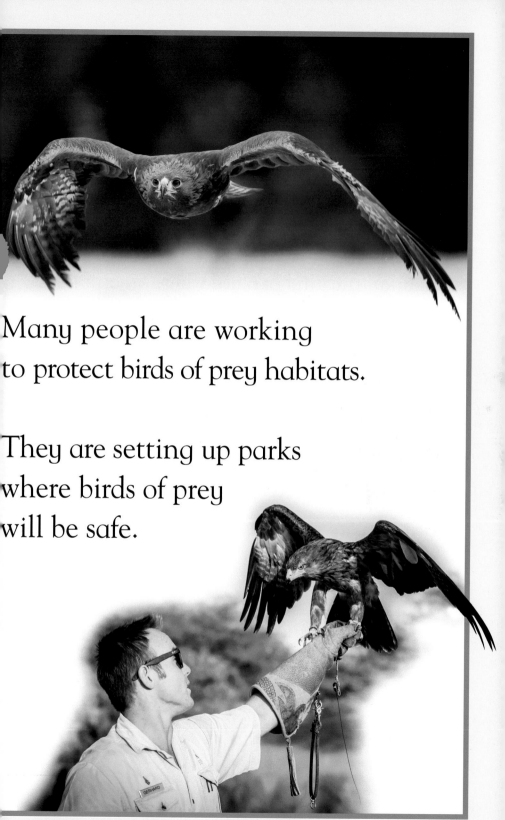

Many people are working
to protect birds of prey habitats.

They are setting up parks
where birds of prey
will be safe.

Glossary

breed to keep animals and help them have babies

carcass the dead body of an animal

grasslands dry, open areas covered in grass

habitat the kind of place where an animal lives

hare an animal that looks like a large rabbit

keen very strong

lemming a small kind of rodent

pests animals that eat and can ruin food that is grown on a farm

prey an animal that is hunted and eaten by other animals

talons sharp claws

vole a small kind of rodent